The 28 Day Shift To Wealth

A Daily Prosperity Plan

Beca Lewis

Perception Publishing

Contents

The 28 Day Shift To Wealth

A Daily Prosperity Plan

If ye have faith as a grain of mustard seed, ye shall say unto this mountain, Remove hence to yonder place; and it shall remove; and nothing shall be impossible unto you.—Matthew 17:20

This 28–Day Journey you are about to take is based on *The Shift System* and the understanding of the law that what you *perceive to be reality magnifies.* This means that what you think or believe is reality will become the day-to-day life that you will experience.

It is not possible to break this law and there is no way around it.

This law can produce terrible cycles in our lives, because the more we believe the worldview, the more we appear to receive it.

If you are experiencing a lack of any kind, unless you break out of the thinking pattern and habits that are producing the movie called Lack, the more lack you will experience.

This law would be scary and discouraging except for one thing.

When your perception shifts to the big R Reality of Divine Love and abundance, the darkness of lack must and will disappear. All belief of lack can be dissolved because it is just a mist—a missed perception—that has no truth other than that we believe it and act out of that belief.

Sometimes we harbor unconscious beliefs that must be uncovered so they can be dissolved, and this book will assist you in doing so.

Your perception does not create anything (good or bad) it just keeps you from seeing what has already been provided.

You are not either a good person or a bad person if you are experiencing lack. Fear of lack and the lie of material sense holds many of us in its grip. But fear can be dissolved forever through the Truth and Principle of Divine Love.

There is no material problem to heal. There is only a belief of a problem. When many people hold that belief, it may appear to be more difficult to dissolve, but it is still just a belief, and can be stepped out of forever.

Sooner or later, we must all escape from the cycle of lack and the worldview of not enough. Sooner or later, we will all have to choose to come out of the belief in a material world and live instead as we are—a Spiritual Being.

In this 28–Day Journey, each day's lesson follows the word **W E A L T H** and includes: a short reading, a mini writing exercise, and a discipline to do for the day.

You can call this work prayer, or meditation, or tasks for the day. It doesn't matter. What matters is that you start the day from the correct premise—the Reality of Good and Abundance—and practice this thinking throughout the day.

You should be able to complete all of this in under 15 minutes a day. The rest of the day is the practice of staying in the point of view and state of mind that you have created in those fifteen minutes.

This practice will shift everything!

If you would like to explore in more depth, the concepts that are mentioned throughout this book, you might like my other books in *The Shift Series*. You will find them listed at the end of this book.

One

Day One

The Truth About WEALTH

Reading For Day One

Understand that wealth is something you already possess. Yes, I know, it rarely feels that way, especially as the worldview is set up to encourage all of us to fear that there is not enough.

Most people succumb to this fear at one time or another, and become obsessed with finding ways to get more—usually money—since that is the currency we most associate with as wealth.

Have you ever noticed that when you are in the fear of not enough and working hard to have enough, there is never enough?

We are going to start from the premise that the *not enough* is a lie. Why?

Because *what you believe to be reality magnifies.* If you and I agree with the worldview that there is not enough, there won't be—for you, for me, for anyone.

To release ourselves, and others, to wealth we all need to: Wake Up! Wake up—Wake Up—the W in W E A L T H.

To see and experience **your** wealth and prosperity, the key is to decide to focus on the wealth already present in your life. Not money. Wealth.

Money will follow when you decide to eliminate any thought that is not about what you and others don't have.

Instead, let's focus entirely on what you do have.

Writing For Day One

Start your *Wealth Journal* today. Spend the next two minutes writing in a journal or this book all the wealth that you can see right now that is already yours to use. Look around, what do you see?

For example: your computer, desk, chair, rug, walls, windows, cup, drink,—keep going!

Discipline For Day One

Did you notice that there is so much wealth right in front of you that you can't possibly write it all down in two minutes!

This is your disciplined thought for today. Repeat to yourself—out loud if possible, as many times as you can—this statement:

"I am awake to wealth!"

How about saying this at least one hundred times today! How about two hundred times? More—yes—you can do it!

Say it while working, playing, brushing your teeth, talking on the phone, watching TV, and driving the car. Turn on the light with this statement. I am awake to wealth!

That's it—simple. You can do it—all day!

"I am awake to wealth!"

Two

Day Two

Waking Up to Wealth - The W in WEALTH

Reading For Day Two

Are you looking for wealth in all the wrong places?

Perhaps you are looking for wealth in your paycheck, your daily sales record, checkbook, bank account, stock market, business, employees, clients, bosses, husband, wife, lottery, or inheritances?

Looking for wealth in these places is like looking for your reflection in the mirror without first standing in the front of the mirror. Obviously, your reflection is only there because you are there.

In the same way, lasting wealth in any form cannot appear until its true substance is seen.

Without knowing its true substance, the wealth you see is only a mirage.

So today let's begin to wake up to the true substance of wealth. This is the wealth that has always been yours and can never be taken away. We are going to start understanding this lasting wealth by beginning the practice of turning things back into thoughts; this is where true substance is found.

How can you do this? You will start by discovering the qualities of the things that you see.

Writing For Day Two

In your *Wealth Journal*, take one thing that you noticed as wealth in your life yesterday and translate it into its true substance by noticing its qualities, and then listing them in your journal. Describe each quality in only one, or maybe two, words.

For example: I could translate the chair I am sitting on to these qualities—useful, comfortable, beautiful, perfect height, well designed, well crafted etc. You are not limited to writing for just two minutes. You can do this for as many things and for as long as you feel like!

Discipline For Day Two

Today, you are going to add extra words to your disciplined thought from yesterday.

You are going to keep this thought in mind, body, and spirit all day: "I am awake to the true substance of wealth!"

You can say it, shout it, or whisper it—just keep it going! If you feel impelled to dance, jump, hop, run or twirl, do that too!

Keep it up—in every moment!

"I am awake to the true substance of wealth!"

Three

Day Three

Waking Up to Wealth -The W In Wealth

Reading For Day Three

As you practice turning things into thoughts, you are not trying to alter a belief. You are not using your mental powers to change physical situations. You are not attempting to blend body, mind, and soul into one.

This is not an exercise in self-will, will power, or even "knowing the truth."

What is it then? It is waking up to the Truth that there is only One Mind—Omnipresent Intelligent Love.

Isn't this a relief producing idea?

Since there is only One Mind, it means that the only creator is the One Mind. It means all-good exists now, everywhere and forever, for you—as you.

Surrender to the One Mind. Give up the struggle. Relax and let yourself experience that you are the Loved of Love.

Writing For Day Three

Today, let's begin the process of discovering what is wealth to you. In your *Wealth Journal,* make a list of things that you believe you want and need in order to feel wealthy. Don't be embarrassed. No one will see this but you. This is not the time to withhold information from yourself, either. Let's get it all out in the open!

Take as long as you want making a list. Not a quality list. We'll get back to that later. Today just list things like cars, homes, clothes, food, money, office items, trips, classes—list it all.

While you are doing this, have fun.

What I don't want you to do is get attached, worried, upset, fearful, depressed, or entertain any negative thoughts about what you don't seem to have while you are making this list.

Pretend you are simply writing a story list, which in fact you are. Play!

Discipline For Day Three

While you are going about your day, notice how many ways the things you have listed that you want already appear in your life.

As you notice them, say this (change the wording to fit for you):

"Thank you for this _____ in my life!"

You may not own most of what you see. It doesn't matter. Be grateful anyway. If you can see it, the idea of it is already present in your awareness. This is where we begin.

Say: *"Thank you for this (car, dress, money ____ all that is on your list) in my life."*

This will be a busy day saying thanks—have fun!

Four

Day Four

Waking Up to Wealth - The W in WEALTH

Reading For Day Four

Are you responsible for making money, finding supply, getting things done? No. Can you really do any of this? Can you make things happen? No.

However, the worldview certainly pressures us to think and act as if we can. The worldview proclaims personal achievement as the goal and working hard as a necessity for getting ahead.

But you are stepping out of the worldview.

You are standing apart from all these beliefs. The worldview of personal power and personal responsibility can not hijack your thoughts, so that all you can think about is a material and physical outcome.

When it feels as if you are responsible, then it may appear that you don't have the time, energy, or desire to practice disciplining thought to God First, which is what we are doing in this course.

But you are awake! You know that your only responsibility is to know Truth and to take action, but only after starting with the correct premise of One Mind.

Instead of being responsible, you are the observer and receiver of the unfolding of all that God Is.

Writing For Day Four

Do you have a wonderful list from yesterday of things that you want? Great! Look at that list and close your eyes. Imagine how it would feel to have all of those things, without work, worry, or responsibility. Imagine that they are present for you now to do as you wish. Then write a quality list of those feelings.

For example:

I would feel:

Free, safe, secure, excited, joyful, etc.

Discipline For Day Four

Pick one of those quality words and say them in the phrase: I AM.

For example:

"I AM freedom."

"I AM safety."

These I AM exercises you are doing are not an affirmation. They are a statement of Truth. There is only One Mind—omnipresent, omnipotent, and omniaction.

When you say I AM, you are speaking as this One Mind. You are waking up to the Truth of yourself.

Note: You can find more about quality lists and how to do them in my book *Living In Grace: The Shift To Spiritual Perception.* or come to *Perceptionu.com* and look for the how-to-do page.

Five

Day Five

Enthusiasm -The E in WEALTH

Reading For Day Five

The 'E' in W E A L T H stands for *enthusiasm*. It is an essential ingredient to seeing and experiencing your wealth and prosperity. The original meaning of the word Enthusiasm is "divine inspiration," or "a god within."

As you have been doing your quality lists for the last four days, you probably have begun to feel divine inspiration.

In essence, you are being Truth by focusing only on what is good, pure, and beautiful.

This is so much easier said than done, especially in the beginning of our practice, because we are all so used to going with the flow of the worldview perception and agreeing with what we see, hear, taste, smell, and touch rather than staying in Truth, which cannot be seen with the five senses.

The key to always seeing and experiencing your wealth and prosperity, is to have a variety of ways that corral your wandering thoughts that drift off to the worldview of lack, limitation, and fear and bring them back to Truth, and what you wish to experience each moment of the day.

Today, you are going to do this by focusing entirely on your qualities of wealth. You are going to *practice seeing the invisible.*

As you do this, expect to feel the divine inspiration of this practice. In fact, practicing seeing the invisible is the most fun you can experience once you get the hang and the habit of it.

Writing For Day Five

Go back to the list you made in your *Wealth Journal* for Day Three.

Pick something on your list. It doesn't matter which one and then turn it into qualities. You are getting to be an expert at this, aren't you?

Make a list of eight to ten qualities. Then write that list on something that you can carry with you for the next few days.

Discipline For Day Five

Take one word on your list and look for examples of this quality in every person, place, or thing that you see today. Start writing these observations in your *Wealth Journa*l.

For example:

If the word *love* is on your quality list, you are going to look for the variety of ways that you see love expressed today.

The idea is to expand your awareness of love, to see that it exists in infinite forms and is always available to you, when you are awake to seeing it.

Be prepared to experience enthusiasm as you do this.

Enthusiasm is you!

Six

Day Six

ENTHUSIASM THE E IN WEALTH

Reading For Day Six

The enthusiasm that we are talking about is not the "jump up and down" kind—although it may inspire this behavior.

It is the internal enthusiasm that comes from divine inspiration. It comes from the internal knowing that no matter what appears in your life, if it is not a result of unlimited Love—it is not Truth.

When those moments, or days, of doubt or fear enter your thoughts and you wonder if there is something wrong with you because you are still in lack of some kind, think about it this way. If you were working a math problem, but just couldn't find the answer, would you assume that the principle behind the correct answer was wrong? No.

In the same way, when Divine Love does not appear to be expressed as abundance in your life, that doesn't make the principle of what you are learning wrong.

As evidence grows in your life that the Principle of Divine Love **does** work, even when it doesn't appear to be working for you, you will still feel Enthusiasm because you know that the Principle is correct, and you will experience the outcome in your life. It only requires faith the size of a mustard seed.

Writing For Day Six

For your two minutes of writing today, simply write about how you are feeling about where you are in life. Express yourself truthfully. Remember, no one will see this but you. Don't worry if some of it is about the negative things that may be going on.

Remember, untruths sometimes have to be uncovered to be dissolved.

When you are finished writing, read what you have written and add a written comment to yourself about it at the end. This observation is critical, so please don't skip this part of the writing assignment.

Discipline For Day Six

Yesterday, you noticed a specific quality in every person, place, or thing. Today, using the same quality word, you will continue to look for this quality with an additional twist.

Every time you notice this quality, express gratitude for its existence in your life. Do this even if it seems to have nothing to do with you. If you noticed it—it does.

Use your own words, but it might sound something like this if love was your quality word:

"Thank you for the love I see expressed as that mother kisses her child, or the love I see as someone tends their garden, or opens the door for another, or" ...you get the idea.

The list is endless, as is Love.

SEVEN

DAY SEVEN

ENTHUSIASM - THE E IN WEALTH

READING FOR DAY SEVEN

Although you were probably not aware of it, in this first week of your 28–Day Shift to Wealth, you have been practicing the first two steps to *The Shift.*

Those first two steps are:

1. *Be Willing*

2. *Become Aware*

When you began this course and started to practice these concepts, you **demonstrated the willingness** to let go of what isn't True and to understand and live Truth.

As you practice the quality words, you **have become more aware** of Divine Love.

One of the most important beliefs we must be willing to let go of is the idea of personality. Any personality; yours, mine, the people in the news, at work, your children, friends, celebrities—everyone.

I know, the worldview holds personality in high esteem. However, personality is what binds us to lack and limitation. Personality is a limited material sense of each one of us. *Be Willing* to let it go.

Become Aware instead of the true essence of each person as the qualities that they uniquely express.

Writing For Day Seven

In your *Wealth Journal,* describe some of the wonderful examples that you have seen of the quality word you are working with and how it felt to be grateful for the experience of it—even when it appeared to be outside your own life.

Discipline For Day Seven

Continue with the same quality word practice not only seeing it everywhere, but practice being it everywhere.

For example: Using the quality word Love:

Ask yourself throughout the day, *"Are my thoughts loving towards others? Are my thoughts loving towards myself? Would Love do this to Itself?"*

Eight

Day Eight

Enthusiasm - The E in WEALTH

Reading For Day Eight

How often does your personality declare to you that you have a right to be sad, miserable, discouraged, depressed, fearful, angry, withdrawn, apathetic, unhappy, listless or any other quality that is the opposite of enthusiasm or joy?

After all, it declares, "Think what you have gone through in your life. Remember how badly this worked out? What about the love you lost? What about your savings that are now gone? Remember how that person betrayed you? Oh yes, what about the people you know who always get ahead but are "bad people?"

See, I don't even have to know you personally to know that some—if not all—of these thoughts occur to you.

Why? Because I know personality, and that personality suggests all these thoughts to each one of us, although perhaps worded differently depending on what style of communication we are used to receiving.

Sure, you can come up with lots of reasons to entertain those kinds of thoughts. People will understand. After all, it makes you "more like them." But succumbing to this temptation won't get you any closer to your desire to understand

and experience the enthusiasm of knowing wealth and prosperity.

Just remember, **you are not your personality; you are so much more,** and that is what you are discovering.

Now—feel that joy!

Discipline For Day Eight

Today you are going to *Become Aware* of whether or not you are *being* the quality word that you have been working with the last few days. Once again, using the quality word of *love* for an example: observe your thoughts and actions throughout the day and ask yourself: "Am I acting as love? Are my thoughts loving towards others? Are my thoughts loving towards myself?"

Be an observer only. No judgment—after all, judgment wouldn't be love, would it?

Writing For Day Eight

This writing takes place after the discipline for the day has gone on for at least a few hours.

Write your observations of how successful or unsuccessful you have been being the quality word of the day.

Write and observe. That's it!

Be Love!

NINE

DAY NINE

ANGEL IDEAS - THE A IN WEALTH

READING FOR DAY NINE

Today is the third letter of W E A L T H in *The 28-Day Shift to Wealth.*

The A in W E A L T H stands for Angel Ideas—those marvelous ideas that seem to pop out of nowhere, bringing light to any situation.

These angel ideas are always immediately available.

In fact, they are ready for you even before you ask for them. They wait for you to listen for them. When you do, they bring you the solution to a problem, an idea for something new, a way to see something differently, and joy to the moment.

Angel ideas are different from human thoughts.

Thoughts can keep us in the worldview by repeating back to us only what appears to be true and then making it appear even more real by giving us a rationalization for why it must be true.

Nothing about human thoughts releases us from our current point of view.

Angel ideas lift us above and out of the worldview. For those people who don't honor angel ideas, they seem "impossible, silly, never been done, how will that work, can I really do those" kinds of ideas.

For those of you who expect, honor, and love angel ideas, know that they are pure wealth.

Discipline For Day Nine

Listen, and expect to hear, and be moved by, innumerable angel ideas.

Expect to revel in the delightful, brilliant light that they bring to every corner of your life. Expect them to dissolve all limitations in the process.

Remember the phrase we all learned before crossing the street when we were kids? "Stop, Look, and Listen." What a perfect reminder. So, before doing anything today—"Stop, Look, and Listen" for angel ideas. They are there—always!

Writing For Day Nine

After you spend the day listening, jot down some of the ideas, and thoughts that come through to you in your *Wealth Journal*. Don't worry about figuring out whether they are thoughts or ideas. We'll address that issue in the next few days. For now, just be a scribe and write them down!

TEN

DAY TEN

ANGEL IDEAS - THE A IN WEALTH

READING FOR DAY TEN

How can you tell the difference between an angel idea and a thought?

Although thinking and thoughts are obviously useful, for our purposes, we want to distinguish between a thought of what to do, and an angel idea of what to do.

An angel idea is what is often called "inspiration."

It appears outside the bounds of what seems possible. A human thought of what to do starts with the premise that you are a material being, and material laws govern your life and control your wealth.

An angel idea will stretch what you think is possible for you.

It will take you out of your material personality and its limitations. A thought of what to do fits what you already know, and in most cases will simply be a band-aid to fix the immediate situation.

An angel idea is not always obvious as to the why of doing something.

In fact, it can be completely unrelated. For example: You begin wondering about how to buy a new house, and the angel idea comes to you to call a friend and find out how they are, or go for a walk in the park, or shine your shoes.

These angel ideas do not seem to relate to the situation. But an angel idea will lead you on a path that will provide in ways you could not think of on your own.

However, this is where it can get tricky. These may be thoughts that are a distraction to keep you from studying and understanding Truth. However, you'll be able to tell the difference as you continue working with quality words.

Keep listening and practicing. As you do so, you will be better able to hear angel ideas and know the difference between them and fear-based human thoughts and distractions.

Writing For Day Ten

Keep writing the angel ideas and thoughts that are coming to you. It's okay to write them both down. Your *Wealth Journal* is a place to record all that you are thinking about.

However, you are also writing how you feel about each Angel Idea or thought, and this will begin the process of uncovering which one it is.

Discipline For Day Ten

Today, would you keep this idea at the forefront of all that you do?

"I am listening and being guided by Angel Ideas."

That's it—you can do it!

ELEVEN

DAY ELEVEN

ANGEL IDEAS - THE A IN WEALTH

READING FOR DAY ELEVEN

As you practice using quality words to turn things back into thoughts, you are practicing tuning into angel ideas.

This process brings your material thinking into the realm of thinking as One Mind. Then, when you need or desire something, an angel idea will be an enlightened message based on Truth.

When you begin with qualities, the objects, the work, your loves, and the people that appear in your life will be more abundant as their true spiritual nature shines through the belief that they are material.

Because angel ideas call for some form of action on your part, the A in W E A L T H can also stand for *action.*

It may be a form of action in which you do something, or it may be a form of action in which it appears that you don't do anything, which I call "active not doing."

Once again, you may ask, "How do I know if it is an angel idea, or a thought based on a material perception?" One way to know is to ask yourself if you feel impelled or compelled. Impel means "to set in motion, move, actuate, drive, mobilize" which is the way an angel idea will guide you.

On the other hand, compel means to "cause a person or thing to yield to pressure, force, oblige, make happen." Compel may cause you to take action based on a material perception.

The action may be the same, but when the basis starts from an angel idea, the outcome will be harmonious and lasting.

Writing For Day Eleven

In your *Wealth Journal,* make a list of actions you have taken in the past that, in retrospect, you can now discern whether it was an Angel Idea or a material perception that motivated you.

Remember to not judge, or succumb to guilt or the "I wish I would have done it better" syndrome. This is observation only!

Discipline For Day Eleven

As you take action and make decisions, pause first and ask yourself, "Do I feel impelled or compelled?"

Take action only on an impel feeling, never on a compel feeling.

Twelve

DayTwelve

Angel Ideas -The A in WEALTH

Reading For Day Twelve

Angel ideas are pure wealth because they instantly connect us to the Truth of our being.

Although we have been talking about angel ideas as if they are telling us to do or not do something, in their purest form, they are statements of Truth; and in that form, they ask nothing of us but to acknowledge Truth.

For example: You are looking for something you misplaced or lost. The angel idea, in this instance, may be the absolute understanding that God is omnipresent.

You might then reason. "How then, could anything be misplaced? How could an omnipresent Mind forget something? Could there ever be a place that omnipresent Mind is not? Therefore, nothing is misplaced or lost—ever."

This idea of omnipresent Mind is the angel idea revealing God.

The result may be a flash of inspiration where the supposedly misplaced object is, or you will see it where it has always been, or it will be replaced or appear in a different manner.

This is inevitable because the material symbol is never the Reality of the object. It is the quality of

God represented by that object which, of course, can never be lost or misplaced.

Writing For Day Twelve

Have you ever lost or misplaced anything?

Turn it back into qualities and write the angel ideas that come to you about the Truth of this thing in your *Wealth Journal.*

Discipline For Day Twelve

Your disciplined statement for the day is:

"I AM omnipresent Mind and Mind never loses or forgets."

Remember to say to yourself as many times as you can; you can write it, sing it, dance it, run it.

Just keep this angel idea in the forefront of your day.

Thirteen

Day Thirteen

Love - The L In WEALTH

Reading For Day Thirteen

It seems obvious, doesn't it? If we have love, we are wealthy. But often we *do* have love and still don't feel wealthy or prosperous.

There is something you can do to increase both Love and your experience of wealth.

You can love.

You can refuse to do anything but see and be love. No matter what the person, place, thing, or situation looks like, you can find something good to love about it. You can refuse to be tempted to discuss, think about, or be afraid of anything that does not appear to be good.

As I wrote this, I was sitting in an airport, and just as I wrote—*you can see only love*—I noticed a woman walk by with her two children and bend to kiss her daughter on the forehead. Love!

Earlier in the day, I experienced a room of over two hundred people extend love—without thinking of anything but love—to a man in trouble. Love was the tangible feeling in the room, and love healed the situation.

If you think about it, you know anytime love is acknowledged, it becomes obvious that love is the only power, and in the moments of experiencing love, you know W E A L T H without measure.

However, instead of seeing love, we are in the habit of discussing the "story of what doesn't, isn't, or won't work."

No longer! You are done with the story of lack, and you are now living only the Truth of love.

Discipline For Day Thirteen

Since you are going to be thinking only about love, you are actually going on a thought diet—instead of a food diet.

Today, you will avoid all those thoughts that are bad for you.

"Magically" it will also affect anyone else within the radiance and radius of your thought.

Imagine that! Others will have the benefit of your diet.

Don't worry about how this thought diet will bring you wealth and prosperity. In fact, that worry is something that you are dieting from today. In this Llove diet you can love every second of the day. Don't hold back. Stuff yourself with love.

Writing For Day Thirteen

Feels good to be full of love, doesn't it? Spend some time today noticing love and writing it in your *Wealth Journa*l. Also note what happens to you and your day when you are only full of love.

FOURTEEN

DAY FOURTEEN

LOVE - THE L IN WEALTH

READING FOR DAY FOURTEEN

I have heard it said that the person you love the least is how much you understand of God—or Divine Love.

This must be true because if we really understood that everything is the creation and outpouring and expression of, and thought of, and love of LOVE—then what is there not to love? How can we say Divine Love is omnipresent and then turn around and see someone or something that is not love?

It can't happen, but it seems to. There appears to be many unloving, unkind, and perhaps evil people doing unloving, unkind, and evil things. In fact, as you continue to live and see only the qualities of love, what is not love will become more apparent.

This is a good thing.

Why? Because what is not love is coming to your attention so that you can dissolve it with Truth.

This doesn't mean you should hang out with it, hoping to cure it. It means you dissolve it by knowing that there is only love. Any action you take from this perfect standpoint will result in the perfect solution to the situation. Listen to those angel ideas—they will guide you.

You are still on the Love diet, so continue to Love—accepting nothing but Love in yourself and others.

Writing For Day Fourteen

Consider the word love and write all the qualities that you can think of that are love to you.

Discipline For Day Fourteen

Here are your two statements for the day. Please say: *"I AM Love"* and then take one of the qualities of Love and say that too. "I AM _____"

All day in every way! Love *is* you!

FIFTEEN

DAY FIFTEEN

LOVE - THE L IN WEALTH

READING FOR DAY FIFTEEN

The second commandment is: "Thou shalt love thy neighbor as yourself." Do you?

Yourself, I mean; do you love yourself? Because, if read correctly, this statement means your neighbor is yourself. So before you can truly love what you perceive as your neighbor, you must love yourself. As you become more and more aware of the fact that you are Love Itself, this loving yourself becomes easier.

In actuality, you are Love Loving Itself.

It sounds nice, doesn't it? Although it is True, if we aren't living it moment-by-moment, it is as illusive as the words on this page. Our intent is to be living Truth.

So today, let's uncover what you **don't** love about yourself. How? By listening to the voice in your head and what you say to yourself.

Before you start this process, know this. **The voice in your head is not you.**

It sounds like you, speaks the way you do, tells you what you think you would say to yourself. But, it's not you. It's the tempter deceiving you into believing something that is not Truth.

Of course it sounds like you because otherwise you wouldn't listen.

This fact will separate you from what it says. However, if you don't know what it is saying, you can't dissolve all of it.

As you listen today, stay in Love. If you do that you might find yourself laughing at the absurdity of the tempter's lies.

Discipline For Day Fifteen

Listen to what the voice in your head is saying to you, and what you say out loud to yourself about yourself, or how you describe yourself to others.

Writing For Day Fifteen:

Write in your *Wealth Journal* what you hear yourself say or think.

Remember, when you discover what isn't good, loving, and pure in yourself and others, always remain an observer knowing this is not Truth about you, or them.

SIXTEEN

DAY SIXTEEN

LOVE - THE L IN WEALTH

READING FOR DAY SIXTEEN

Today, let's gather wisdom about love from the words of a poet long ago; substituting the word love for the word charity to arrive at the original meaning.

"*And now I will show you the most excellent way.*

If I have the gift of prophecy and can fathom all mysteries and all knowledge and if I have a faith that can move mountains, but have not love, I am nothing.

If I give all I possess to the poor and surrender my body to the flames, but have not love, I gain nothing.

Love is patient. Love is kind. It does not envy, it does not boast, it is not proud.

It is not rude, it is not self-seeking, it is not easily angered, it keeps no record of wrongs. Love does not delight in evil but rejoices with the truth.

It always protects, always trusts, always hopes, always perseveres. Love never fails. And now these three remain: faith, hope and love. But the greatest of these is love." — Corinthians 13

Discipline For Day Sixteen

What a perfect description of love. As you can see, this passage states the qualities of Love, and the action of love, based on these qualities.

Make a list of the qualities and actions of love found in the poem and put the list where you can see it today.

Throughout the day, ask yourself if you are acting as love in all these ways.

Also, be aware of those who claim to love, but are not being, or acting, from these qualities.

Once again, be an observer only and stay with the Truth of being in every instant.

Writing For Day Sixteen

Write a *love letter* to yourself!

Make it a wonderful letter full of appreciation and acknowledgement and all the qualities found in the poem we are reading today.

Put the letter in an envelope and date it a year from now. Put it somewhere you will see it next year so you can read your Love letter from yourself, or perhaps have someone mail it to you.

Seventeen

Day Seventeen

Thanks - The T In WEALTH

Reading For Day Seventeen

What a privilege to be able to say *thanks,* but how often do you do it? Very seldom! I know this to be true, because there are so many things for which all of us forget to be thankful.

I'll prove it.

Stop right now and look around you. Really look. No matter where you are, there are countless things that have been provided for you.

For example: I know everyone of you is reading these words. Think of that. Think of the millions of events that have taken place that have made it possible for you to be able to read this message wherever you are, written by me on my computer, wherever I am living.

Imagine what has been provided for you in order for this to happen; the electricity, the software, the paper, the printing, etc.

Think of the dedication, energy, love, and care that so many people have given to each element of what we all so casually use.

You could spend hours giving thanks just for the things you are aware of within the circle of your arms.

I know another thing that you are not thankful enough for—the talents that have been given to you.

No matter how good you are at giving thanks for them, I know you have missed a few. Most of us have missed almost all of them. To rediscover your talents, start small.

Once again, start where you are sitting. What are you doing?

Think of the gifts and talents you have been given that allow you to do that.

Expand out into your day, then your community.

Notice how you express unlimited talent and gifts each second of the day.

Writing For Day Seventeen

Take time to list in your *Wealth Journal* all the talents you have noticed.

Don't forget to say thanks for each one! When you are done—think again—I am positive there are more!

Discipline For Day Seventeen

Give *thanks* today.

Give *thanks* out loud when an Angel Idea moves you to speak.

Give *thanks* inside for everything. Remember, we are seeing what has been given, and today we give *thanks*.

I am giving *thanks* for you and your unique gifts and talents that you share with the world.

Thank you!

Eighteen

Day Eighteen

Thanks - The T In WEALTH

Reading For Day Eighteen

Amid the claim of lack—which produces worry, anxiety, and fear—we can be thankful that the claim of lack is a lie. We can be thankful that in Truth there is only One Creator and One Power, only one Intelligent Loving Mind and we are the Loved of this Love, and all that It is and has, we are, and we have.

We can say thank you for the Truth, even if there are times it doesn't appear to be true to us. We can do this in the same way we can say thank you for the fact that the earth is round although appearing flat, for the fact that railroad tracks don't merge in the distance even though it appears that they do, for the fact that all that we see is mostly space even though it appears solid.

All these material symbols show us that what we see, hear, taste and touch is not Truth—it is perception.

We can therefore be grateful and give thanks for the fact that no matter what current material perceptions may suggest, we know that spiritual perception will reveal all our needs provided for, before we knew we had a need.

It's a spiritual law. *"Seek ye first the Kingdom of God and his righteousness: and all these things shall be added unto thee."*— Matthew 6:33

We can be thankful that our desire is to *Seek ye first the Kingdom of God* and rest in the assurance that all these things have already been provided. We can be thankful for the Truth that we can and will perceive their presence now.

Writing For Day Eighteen

Spend your two minutes today beginning a gratitude list, and writing a thank you note to Divine Love.

Discipline For Day Eighteen

Stay in gratitude and thankfulness for your permanent, unlimited wealth, no matter what the temptation is to believe otherwise.

NINETEEN

DAY NINETEEN

THANKS - THE T IN WEALTH

READING FOR DAY NINETEEN

Does it concern you that there appears to be lack for others? Is this one of the thoughts that has been binding you to the belief of lack?

There appears to be a tremendous amount of poverty in the world, and we hear about it all the time. It appears in the news about other countries, or on the streets of our hometown. Sometimes this poverty strikes closer to home as it appears in our children, parents, and friends.

These pictures of poverty, whether on TV, the news, a phone call, or a letter from a loved one, touches the emotions of our heart and pulls us into the worldview of lack by suggesting that poverty exists for them.

If it doesn't exist for you, it doesn't exist for anyone—anywhere—anytime. Whenever these pictures of poverty appear—in whatever form—we must be diligent in rejecting them.

Not ignoring them. Rejecting them!

Think of it this way. If you were in a theatre watching a movie and someone you know was an actor in the movie playing a homeless person, would you then rush home to see what you could do to make sure they were clothed and fed? Of course not. You would know that in Truth they were secure and safe.

In the same way, when we are presented with the movie of poverty and lack for others, we can know this is a material perception and therefore not true. Using spiritual perception, we can know that all the people we see in poverty are really, just as you are, safe, secure, and lovingly provided for by Divine Love.

As the mist dissolves, the worldview of lack will also dissolve.

In the meantime, when you start with the correct spiritual perception, any action that you take to express love to those who appear to be in need, will not only be practical, but will also bring the spiritual light which can lift them too from the illusion of lack.

Remember, what you see is really what you believe. The dreamer and the dream are one.

Think how wonderful it will be as we begin to perceive as Divine Love perceives!

Writing For Day Nineteen

You have been writing about what you are grateful for in your life. Today spend some time writing a gratitude list for what has been provided to others.

Discipline For Day Nineteen

When presented with the illusion of lack, for anyone, do not agree with it.

Do not sympathize with it.

While bringing empathy to the situation, stay in the knowledge of One Mind—Divine Love pre-providing all that each person needs or desires.

Twenty

Day Twenty

Thanks - The T In WEALTH

Reading For Day Twenty

Have you ever stopped to realize that **you** are supply? Think about all that you are and all that you do and how much you are a supply to others.

It's not just that you may be bringing an income to a family; it is much more than that.

It's a smile, a touch, and an acknowledgement. It's your kindness, attention, hugs, and readiness to help.

Your unique expression of Divine Love and the One Mind is endless supply in a multitude of ways. This is something for which you can be thankful.

Be thankful that your purpose is innate, that you are invaluable and an inevitable supply, without trying to make it happen. Be thankful that there is nothing for you to do except surrender to being your unique expression and take action as directed by angel ideas.

Writing For Day Twenty

Today write in your *Wealth Journal* in what ways you are supply for others. If you really don't know—ask!

Discipline for Day Twenty

Your statement for the day: “I AM supply.” As the day’s events continue around you, stay in this thought: “I AM supply.”

Twenty-One

Day Twenty One

Help -The H In WEALTH

Reading For Day Twenty-One

When I first heard the angel idea of using the word WEALTH, I thought the H was for *help others*. When I listened again, I realized that the H in help means: "Help yourself first."

Before you can effectively help others, you must help yourself.

You are now. You are taking the time to redirect your thinking—to shift your perceptions, to know the truth about wealth, because if you understand wealth, you will have it and be able to share it.

But what about other times?

Have you ever found yourself distracting yourself from your true wishes and passion by helping others before you helped yourself? Isn't this action one of the most draining, stifling, and ultimately wealth stealing things you can do?

Yes, it is, and in the end, you have nothing left to help others with—no desires, no motivation, no resources. Sometimes we use this lack as a weapon against others. (For example: 'I gave up all my dreams for you.')

So today, you can ask yourself first, *"How can I help you?"*

Helping yourself first may take just a moment of thought shifting, or it may take many days, weeks, or months. However, when you start with helping yourself first, you will find you will naturally move out into the world and ask, "*How can I help you?*"

You will be so filled with wealth that sharing and using it will become your nature. Your desire to help will expand into a dream bigger than yourself that will become the motive of your days and will outlive your personal time on earth.

Therefore, no matter how much you help others now, stop and help yourself first, and then let that flow out of you into whatever action angel ideas lead you to do.

Discipline For Day Twenty-One

Your disciplined thought for the day is to ask yourself this question: "*How can I help you?*"

Writing For Day Twenty-One

When you hear the answers to that question, write them down in your *Wealth Journal.*

This will be an invaluable aid in remembering that supply is you.

Helping yourself first is one of the primary ways to say "thank you" for the gift of wealth that is you.

Twenty-Two

Day Twenty Two

Help - The H In WEALTH

Reading For Day Twenty-Two:

Have you ever needed help but not asked for it? Why? Perhaps it was because you were embarrassed, ("I should know better") afraid, ("they will be so angry or upset with me"), indifferent ("what difference will it make anyway"), "good reasons" ("I don't have the time, money, patience, knowledge, contacts etc.").

Do any of these reasons sound like an angel idea leading you to light and love? No, they sound like the "tempter" lying to you about who you are and what is true wealth.

Help is a built in provision of supply and wealth.

Look at the many symbols of this idea of supply found in nature. The sun helps us all, the wind spreads seeds and clears the air, the rain supplies needed moisture for all life.

It's a reciprocal law of being.

When you ask for help someone is now free to give you that help. Perhaps their greatest wish is to be of service, or perhaps they have yet to learn of the gift of service.

Either way, your asking for help allows them to be supply, and you to surrender your personality to your true nature as an expression of Divine Love.

Discipline For Day Twenty-Two

Ask someone for help. Simple. No rules—just ask.

Writing For Day Twenty-Two

Sometimes this asking for help is to make use of services, ideas, classes, meetings, and gifts already available to you.

Make a list in your *Wealth Journal* of any kind of supply of help that you already know about, but haven't yet used. If one is appropriate for your current need, then go get it and use it.

Twenty-Three

Day Twenty Three

Help - The H In WEALTH

Reading For Day Twenty-Three

If you asked for help yesterday, someone responded. Did you notice?

Did you remember to give thanks for their help? Giving thanks is a vital part of the circle of reciprocal being.

Give thanks with what you have, knowing you have an unlimited supply.

Now that you are helping yourself first and are in the habit of asking for help—you are aren't you—you can move on in the circle. You can pass it on. You can be of help and service to many. You don't need an acknowledgement or reward for being of service.

You are not giving help to be a good person, but to express yourself as a spiritual being.

However, when you help others, you are not providing a way for them to continue in any behavior that does not serve them. The first step in helping others is knowing who they really are—Spiritual—and then treating them as if that was true.

True help does not keep anyone in a position of helplessness.

Help supplies the need with love, and with the expectation that their need is temporary. The greatest help you can give another is to hold to the unwavering knowledge about their true spiritual nature.

No matter what they believe about themselves, you can know and love them as they truly are.

Discipline For Day Twenty-Three

Your disciplined thoughts for the day are:

"I am aware and grateful for the abundant help that I am continually receiving. I am aware of the need of others and I am grateful to be able to provide it as the expression of Divine Love."

Writing For Day Twenty-Three

What help have you received in the last twenty-four hours?

Think about it.

Help arrives in a multitude of ways, if you will but look. This could be an ongoing list in your *Wealth Journal.*

Thank you for helping others as you help yourself!

Twenty-Four

Day Twenty Four

Help - The H In WEALTH

Reading For Day Twenty-Four

What is the best help you can give to yourself, and therefore to others today?

You can step outside of the material picture.

You can choose to not identify with any suggestion of lack in yourself or others.

No matter what the material picture is telling you about what you don't have, or what you need, you can choose to remain in the internal knowledge of the truth of constant, loving, and practical supply.

When human hope fades, you can help yourself by remembering good is the only power. You can remind yourself how often you have proven this to yourself in your own life, and heard and read about the proofs of good in other's lives.

You can help yourself by remembering the power and truth of Elisha's statement, "*Fear not: for they that be with us are more than they that be with them.*"—II Kings 6:16

You can help yourself by remaining constantly aware of the still small place within—listening only to the voice of wisdom found in this stillness.

You can help yourself by letting go of how you think it "should" be and know only that God is in control and has already provided all that you need.

You can help yourself by not listening to, reading, talking, or entertaining any thoughts that do not declare the eternal, omnipotent power of Divine Love Loving you as Its own.

Discipline For Day Twenty-Four

Today your eternal and still thought is: *"I Am the Loved of Love."*

Writing For Day Twenty-Four

Look back on your life for proofs of good and spend your two minutes today recording them in your *Wealth Journal.*

Write: *"I Am the Loved of Love"* throughout the day on whatever is nearby to write on.

TWENTY-FIVE

DAY TWENTY FIVE

THE FINAL STEPS - PRACTICE

W=Wake Up, **E**=Enthusiasm, **A**=Angel Ideas, **L**=Love, **T**=Thanks, **H**=Help

READING FOR DAY TWENTY-FIVE

Yes, we have covered all the letters in the word W E A L T H!

But there is one more step in the process. And that is the vital step of practice.

While writing this section of the book, Del and I moved to an apartment in town for the summer. While making arrangements with the landlord, I noticed that it looked as if a garden had once been planted around the house, but had become choked with weeds.

When I mentioned this to her, she suggested that perhaps I would like to take care of the garden for the summer. After a bit of negotiation, I got the job.

At first, it looked as if it would only take a few hours to clean the garden. But I was wrong. It took a very long time, and it was very hard work.

As I hoed and weeded, it occurred to me what a perfect metaphor gardening is for what we are studying.

Underneath all the weeds, it was possible to see that someone originally cared enough to buy expensive and beautiful plants. And then they neglected them so that most of them died, or became the bare bones of what they once were, showing very little beauty.

For the past twenty-four days, you have taken precious time and care to plant a beautiful *thought garden.*

But without continued, constant care, it too will be overgrown with the weeds of the old habits of perception and aggressiveness of the worldview.

When our landlord first planted the garden, it must have looked beautiful. But she stopped too soon. If she had taken just a bit more time to cover the soil with the weed stopping fabric or cardboard, and then mulch, not only would very few weeds have grown, but the plants she wanted would also have thrived, providing enjoyment for all—and eliminating all the work of restoration.

In the same way, you must cover the soil of your thinking with the protective understanding of Truth and continue to mulch and water your thoughts with the nutriment of Divine Love.

It takes constant practice. But you know that practice is as important as planting in the first place.

Writing For Day Twenty-Five

Imagine what you have been studying for the last twenty-four days is a garden and describe it to yourself in your *Wealth Journal*.

Discipline For Day Twenty-Five

Notice if any old thought habits have crept back in, and uproot them immediately, before they have time to make deep roots.

TWENTY-SIX

DAY TWENTY SIX

THE FINAL STEPS - PRACTICE

W=Wake Up, **E**=Enthusiasm, **A**=Angel Ideas, **L**=Love, **T**=Thanks, **H**=Help

READING FOR DAY TWENTY-SIX

The premise that this W E A L T H Course is based on is that there in only One Mind and it is omnipresent, omniscient, omnipotent, omniaction. It is all Intelligent and all Loving.

It is the only Cause and the only Creator.

On the surface, it may appear that you are studying this *Wealth Course* because you want more money, love, happiness, peace, security, time—all the things that most of us never seem to have enough of.

And it is a good thing to expect to have all that you need at all times.

However, you must remember that these things will be the inevitable result of choosing and living the spiritual perception of One Mind. Your desire is to release all the beliefs that hold you in the material world so that you can experience—here and now—heaven on earth.

When you fully realize that what appears as the outside world is really your own perception of reality and the worldview that you have agreed to believe, it makes absolute sense to spend time understanding Reality—first and foremost during every moment of the day.

Easier said than done! But it **must** be done!

I have come up with a few ideas that help me remember to practice during the day so that I don't reach the end of the day and wonder where my thoughts have been.

One that works well is an *oven timer day*.

I spend time studying spiritual perception and when I am done, I set the oven timer, or phone timer, or computer time for forty-five minutes in which I do other things that I feel need to be done. When the timer goes off, I stop whatever I am doing and study some more. Do this for a day or two and notice the difference in the quality of your day.

Discipline For Day Twenty-Six

Use the *oven timer* day method, or choose a method of your own, but stop whatever you are doing every forty-five minutes today and remember that there is only One Mind. This could be a quiet meditation, a time of study, or a moment of prayer.

Writing For Day Twenty-Six

Write in your *Wealth Journal* what attempts to distract you as you take your time to remember? Do you easily stop what you are doing? Awareness is the first step in releasing and dissolving all that is not One Mind.

TWENTY-SEVEN

DAY TWENTY SEVEN

THE FINAL STEPS – PRACTICE

W=Wake Up, **E**=Enthusiasm, **A**=Angel Ideas, **L**=Love, **T**=Thanks, **H**=Help

READING FOR DAY TWENTY-SEVEN

Does practice mean that you are practicing being a better human? Does it mean that you are practicing to "get more spiritual?" Does it mean that you have to make something happen, get better at something or do something to be sure everything works out?

None of these reasons are why you are practicing.

Right now, you are perfect.

Right now, you are a spiritual being with no humanness at all. Right now you are the effect of the One Cause and Creator. Right now you are the embodiment of all that God is. Which means of course that right now you are all the varied forms of wealth that you desire to experience.

So why practice? Until every moment of our day is the expression of this Truth; until our thinking is only God's thinking, until we have only the perception of Reality, we practice. We practice to wake up and to keep our thinking in Truth.

What a glorious awakening it will be when this is no longer necessary because we are fully awake and aware of who we really are: the effect of divine Love and the Infinite One Mind.

In the meantime—we practice—and experience the joy this brings, and the tag along result of what appears to be an improved human experience, which is in reality the veil of mist-perception rolled away and Truth revealed.

Discipline For Day Twenty-Seven

Your constant statement, thought, and motivation for action today is, "*I am the effect of Divine Love and the Infinite One Mind.*"

Writing For Day Twenty-Seven

As the effect and embodiment of Divine Love and the Infinite One Mind, write in your *Wealth Journal* how life *really* is for you.

Twenty-Eight

Day Twenty Eight

The Final Steps - Practice

W=Wake Up, **E**=Enthusiasm, **A**=Angel Ideas, **L**=Love, **T**=Thanks, **H**=Help

Reading For Day Twenty-Eight

For the past twenty-eight days, we have practiced together. We learned how to use the word W E A L T H as our guide.

During these last twenty-eight days, you have increased your understanding of **True Wealth**.

You have done this because you know that when you understand this wealth, you will never worry about lack again. Now that you have started this process, don't stop!

Continue to practice the Truth about Wealth, just as you practice any other skill. Some days will feel easier than others, but the results will far outweigh any discomfort along the way.

What this practice will reveal to you is the treasure that can never be taken from you. A treasure that you can spend with the assurance that it will never be depleted.

Never worry about the outcome of what you are guided to do.

That is not your job. You can't control what other people say, think, or do. Your job is to start with the correct premise in your own thinking and to constantly pay attention to your motive for all the actions you take or don't take.

If you discover that you don't always walk in True Wealth (none of us do yet) be thankful for that awareness and then let it go.

Never hold on to those things you discover about yourself that are not beautiful and loving. Don't say to yourself, "this is who I am," don't beat yourself up for your mistakes, big or small. Let them go.

Set yourself free to be and experience True Wealth.

I know that you are walking now in the light of the Truth about Wealth and I am privileged to have been able to spend this time with you!

Wealth is You!

Discipline For Day Twenty-Eight

Today your eternal thought is: "*I Am Love Loving Itself.*" Repeat this constantly to yourself throughout the day.

Writing For Day Twenty-Eight

Look back on your life for proofs of good and spend your two minutes today recording them in your *Wealth Journal.*

Write: "*I Am the Loved of Love*" throughout the day on whatever is nearby to write on.

Twenty-Nine

Keep Going

It's so easy to forget or slip back into the worldview of lack and limitation. There is so much agreement about *not enough* or *not good enough* that it takes a conscious, consistent commitment of thought to stay in W E A L T H.

Without that conscious, consistent commitment of thought and action—habit takes over.

If habit were a person, it would be someone who waits outside your door every minute of the day, and when you open that door just a tiny bit, it uses all its force to push its way into your home.

Then it moves your stuff around the room to suit itself, sits down in the most comfortable place in the room, and starts telling everyone else how it is going to be, starting now and forever.

If you find that habit of accepting the worldview of lack making itself at home again in your thinking, there is only one way to get it out.

No—pushing or begging won't work. Arguing about what is True won't move that habit.

Although arguing for what is True can be useful because it increase the strength in us to do the only thing that will banish that habit.

And that is to **turn on the light!!**

It's easy, isn't it? Because what's hard is remembering to keep the door shut and remembering to turn on the light. Habit makes us forgetful.

So two thoughts for today: **Keep the door of your thinking shut to the beliefs of lack and limitation and keep that light shining!**

It takes a complete, conscious commitment to **not** become hypnotized by the continuing demands of lack, to believe in it whichever form it takes. No matter how loudly the voice of lack may scream, it can be silenced by knowing its power is your reaction to it and your belief in it.

Use the W E A L T H system to shatter these dark thoughts with the power of light.

This is not a passive state; it is an active state. Now is the time to join the millions of people who desire to see peace and wealth for every individual.

Lack screams loudly to get a reaction from us. When we do not react at all, but instead shine the light of Truth with calmness and Love, the results are amazing.

It doesn't matter how big the problem seems to be, or how little. It is the same problem. It is the belief that we are separated from our source, and that there is a power other than Good.

Don't believe it. It doesn't matter if, at the moment, we don't understand this, but we don't have to believe the lie. This is imperative in your personal life. It is imperative for the planet.

Will you take a moment today to see yourself as Light?

Pretend that you are unzipping your human covering and inside is Light. Unzip and let it pour out. Let it dissolve any darkness it touches.

Send that light to shatter any dark beliefs that you find existing in your thought or the world's thought.

You are the light!

Author Note

Thank you for reading my books! I write for you. If you like what I write, you can help spread the word, and keep my work going, by "liking" anywhere the option is offered.

I would be honored if you would also post your honest reviews of the book. This will help other readers decide whether it is worth their reading time.

Join my mailing list at becalewis.com and get whatever book or book I am giving away for free and discover what else I am up to.

I am looking forward to getting to know you!

-Beca

Also By Beca

The Ruby Sisters Series: Women's Lit, Friendship

A Last Gift, After All This Time, And Then She Remembered...

Stories From Doveland: Magical Realism, Friendship

Karass, Pragma, Jatismar, Exousia, Stemma, Paragnosis,

In-Between, Missing, Out Of Nowhere

The Return To Erda Series: Fantasy

Shatterskin, Deadsweep, Abbadon, The Experiment

The Chronicles of Thamon: Fantasy

Banished, Betrayed, Discovered, Wren's Story

The Shift Series: Spiritual Self-Help

Living in Grace: The Shift to Spiritual Perception

The Daily Shift: Daily Lessons From Love To Money

The 4 Essential Questions: Choosing Spiritually Healthy Habits

The 28 Day Shift To Wealth: A Daily Prosperity Plan

The Intent Course: Say Yes To What Moves You

Imagination Mastery: A Workbook For Shifting

Your Reality

Right Thinking: A Thoughtful System for Healing

Perception Mastery: Seven Steps To Lasting Change

Blooming Your Life: How To Experience Consistent Happiness

Perception Parables: Very short stories

Love's Silent Sweet Secret: A Fable About Love

Golden Chains And Silver Cords: A Fable About Letting Go

Advice:

A Woman's ABC's of Life: Lessons in Love, Life, and Career from Those Who Learned The Hard Way

Other Places To Find Beca

- Facebook: https://www.facebook.com/becalewiscreative
- Instagram: https://instagram.com/becalewis
- TikTok: https://tiktok.com/@becalewis
- Twitter: http://twitter.com/becalewis

- LinkedIn: https://linkedin.com/in/becalewis
- Youtube: https://www.youtube.com/c/becalewis

About Beca

Beca writes books she hopes will change people's perceptions of themselves and the world, and open possibilities to things and ideas that are waiting to be seen and experienced.

At sixteen, Beca founded her own dance studio. Later, she received a Master's Degree in Dance in Choreography from UCLA and founded the Harbinger Dance Theatre, a multimedia dance company, while continuing to run her dance school.

After graduating—to better support her three children—Beca switched to the sales field, where she worked as an employee and independent contractor to many industries, excelling in each while perfecting and teaching her Shift® system, and writing books.

She joined the financial industry in 1983 and became an Associate Vice President of Investments at a major stock brokerage firm, and was a licensed Certified Financial Planner for over twenty years.

This diversity, along with a variety of life challenges, helped fuel the desire to share what she's learned by writing and speaking, hoping it will make a difference in other people's lives.

Beca grew up in State College, PA, with the dream of becoming a dancer and then a writer. She carried that dream forward as she fulfilled a childhood wish by moving to Southern California in 1968. Beca told her family she would never move back to the cold.

After living there for thirty-one years, she met her husband Delbert Lee Piper, Sr., at a retreat in Virginia, and everything changed. They decided to find a place they could call their own, which sent them off traveling around the United States. They lived and worked in a few different places before returning to live in the cold once again near Del's family in a small town in Northeast Ohio, not too far from State College.

When not working and teaching together, they love to visit and play with their combined family of eight children and five grandchildren, read, study, do yoga or taiji, feed birds, and work in their garden.

Other Places To Find Beca

- Facebook: https://www.facebook.com/becalewiscreative
- Instagram: https://instagram.com/becalewis
- TikTok: https://tiktok.com/@becalewis
- Twitter: http://twitter.com/becalewis

- LinkedIn:

  https://linkedin.com/in/becalewis

- Youtube:

  https://www.youtube.com/c/becalewis

Printed in Great Britain
by Amazon

17025545R00081